HISTORY'S CONSPIRACY THEORIES

by Tammy Gagne

12 STORY LIBRARY

www.12StoryLibrary.com

12-Story Library is an imprint of Bookstaves.

Photographs ©: Efrain Padro/Alamy Stock Photo, cover, 1; John Taylor/PD, 4; PD, 5; peresanz/Shutterstock.com, 6; BigAlBaloo/Shutterstock.com, 6; Charles Robinson/PD, 7; Oscar Gustave Rejlander/PD, 7; F.G.O. Stuart/PD, 8; Library of Congress, 9; Chronicle/Alamy Stock Photo, 10; Library of Congress, 11; Roswell Daily Record/PD, 11; Walt Cisco, Dallas Morning News/PD, 12; Everett Collection Inc/Alamy Stock Photo, 13; NASA/Neil A. Armstrong, 15; Pictorial Press Ltd/Alamy Stock Photo, 16; Katie Rommel-Esham/CC3.0, 17; Metro-Goldwyn-Mayer, Inc./Library of Congress, 18; Cybjorg/CC3.0, 19; mark reinstein/Shutterstock.com, 20; Joao Silva/Associated Press, 21; Jeffmock/CC3.0, 22; TSGT CEDRIC H. RUDISILL/US Air Force, 23; Pete Souza, The Obama-Biden Transition Project/CC3.0, 24; State of Hawaii Department of Health/PD, 25; PD, 25; US Department of Energy, 26; US Food and Drug Administration, 27; Anton_Ivanov/Shutterstock.com, 28; Library of Congress, 29

ISBN
978-1-63235-590-4 (hardcover)
978-1-63235-644-4 (paperback)
978-1-63235-703-8 (ebook)

Library of Congress Control Number: 2018938108

Printed in the United States of America
Mankato, MN
July 2018

About the Cover

Flying saucer and aliens exhibit at the UFO Museum in Roswell, New Mexico.

12 STORY LIBRARY

Access free, up-to-date content on this topic plus a full digital version of this book. Scan the QR code on page 31 or use your school's login at 12StoryLibrary.com.

Table of Contents

1

Shakespeare Didn't Write His Own Plays

37

Number of plays that Shakespeare is said to have written.

- William Shakespeare is known in history as a famous playwright.
- Not much is known about his life.
- Some people have claimed that other people wrote Shakespeare's plays.
- No one has been able to prove or disprove the conspiracy theories about Shakespeare.

William Shakespeare is one of the best-known playwrights in history. Three of his most famous plays are *Romeo and Juliet, Hamlet,* and *Macbeth*. But some people believe that Shakespeare didn't write them.

Shakespeare was born in England around 1564. He was an actor and a playwright. He married, had children, and owned property. He became famous in the London theater world. He died in 1616. Not much else is known about his life.

Some conspiracy theories claim that Edward de Vere wrote

MORE THAN ONE AUTHOR?

One theory says that many people wrote Shakespeare's plays. In 1848, an American named Joseph C. Hart wrote a book about this theory. In 1856, Delia Bacon wrote an article about it. This has become one of the more popular beliefs among conspiracy theorists.

Shakespeare's plays. De Vere was the 17th Earl of Oxford. An earl is a British nobleman. Many of Shakespeare's plays are about kings, queens, and other royalty. Some people think a common man like Shakespeare wouldn't know about such things. But someone like de Vere would.

Other theories say Sir Francis Bacon wrote the plays. Still others say it was another playwright, Christopher Marlowe. Or they say it was a different earl, William Stanley.

No one yet has been able to prove that Shakespeare didn't write his plays. But no one has been able to prove he wrote them, either.

2

Lewis Carroll Was Jack the Ripper

Alley in Whitechapel, London, the district where Jack the Ripper committed his crimes.

In 1888, a serial killer terrorized London. He murdered at least five women. But he was never caught or even identified. He was called Jack the Ripper.

This case has led to many conspiracy theories. One of the strangest theories claims the elusive killer was a man named Charles Lutwidge Dodgson. He was better known by his pen name, Lewis Carroll. He was the author of *Alice's Adventures in Wonderland.*

Carroll was also a photographer. He took many pictures of young girls. One of these girls, Alice Liddell, was said to inspire *Alice in Wonderland.* Some people who have studied Carroll's life say he did not treat these girls with respect.

Other people have pointed out anagrams in Carroll's writing. When they rearrange some of

THINK ABOUT IT

If the London murders took place today, do you think police would identify and catch the killer? Why or why not?

the letters, messages appear. The messages seem to suggest that Carroll was Jack the Ripper. Some people think this is silly. They argue that with enough letters, nearly anything can be spelled out.

The killings took place more than 130 years ago. But the conspiracy theory about Lewis Carroll lives on.

176

Number of languages into which *Alice in Wonderland* has been translated.

- A man people call Jack the Ripper killed five women in London in 1888.
- One conspiracy theory says that Lewis Carroll was the killer.
- People have based this theory on anagrams.
- Some people still believe Carroll was Jack the Ripper.

Lewis Carroll in 1863.

3

The *Titanic* Didn't Sink

On April 10, 1912, a giant ship called *Titanic* left England for New York City. The owners bragged that the ship was unsinkable. But they were wrong. Four days after departing Southampton, *Titanic* hit an iceberg in the Atlantic Ocean. Less than three hours later, it sank. More than half the people on board lost their lives in the frigid waters.

A conspiracy theory says that *Titanic* did not sink. People who accept this theory believe that a ship went down on the morning of April 15. Wreckage has been found on the ocean floor. But they think *Titanic* wasn't the ship that sank.

This theory suggests that a ship called *Olympic* was used for the fatal voyage. The two vessels were swapped as part of an insurance scam. *Olympic* had a history of collisions.

The *Titanic* on April 10, 1912.

The *Olympic* in 1911.

The ships' owners wanted to get rid of it.

A researcher and author named Robin Gardiner spent much of his life trying to prove this theory. He wrote books about it. One is called *Titanic: The Ship That Never Sank*. It came out in 1998. Another book called *The Great Titanic Conspiracy* followed in 2010.

WAS *TITANIC* UNSINKABLE?

What if this theory is true? Then history's most famous ocean disaster might never have happened. Many people who believe the ships were swapped say the real *Titanic* would have survived hitting the iceberg. Many lives could have been spared that night.

1,500

Number of people who died when *Titanic* sank.

- A ship called *Titanic* departed England for New York City on April 10, 1912.
- It sank four days later after hitting an iceberg.
- Wreckage from the enormous vessel has been found at the bottom of the Atlantic Ocean.
- Conspiracy theories say another ship, *Olympic*, went down that night.

4 A Spaceship Crash-Landed in Roswell, New Mexico

The debris found in a rancher's sheep pasture in 1947.

People have claimed to see unidentified flying objects (UFOs) for many years. A popular theory says that UFOs are spaceships flown to Earth by aliens. But no one has been able to prove that a UFO is a visitor from another planet.

In 1947, a rancher outside Roswell, New Mexico, found debris in his sheep pasture. Soon after, the US Air Force said the wreckage was from a crashed weather balloon. These special balloons contain instruments that measure air conditions. But not everyone believed the Air Force's story. Many people were sure the object was a spaceship. They thought the government didn't want the people to know about it.

Many years later, the government admitted that the debris was part of a top secret project. It was called Project Mogul. Its purpose was to detect Soviet nuclear bomb tests. To this day, many people think the government is covering up an alien landing. They even think the government has a secret spot where they keep the crashed spacecraft and its crew. It is called Area 51.

90

Percent of UFO sightings that can easily be explained.

- UFOs are unidentified flying objects that some people think are alien spaceships.
- In 1947, a rancher in Mexico found strange debris on his land.
- The Air Force said the debris was from a weather balloon.
- The government later admitted the debris was from a secret government project.

Roswell Daily Record

RECORD PHONES
Business Office 2288
News Department 2287

RAAF Captures Flying Saucer On Ranch in Roswell Region

Claims Army Is Stacking Courts Martial

House Passes Tax Slash by Large Margin

Security Council Paves Way to Talks On Arms Reductions

No Details of Flying Disk Are Revealed

Ex-King Carol Weds Mme. Lupescu

Miners and Operators Sign Highest Wage Pact in History

American League Wins All-Star Game

Satellites
ris Meeting

A National Weather Service weather balloon.

5

The Assassination of John F. Kennedy

Four US presidents have been assassinated while serving in office. One of them was John F. Kennedy. He was shot during a visit to Dallas, Texas, on November 22, 1963. Shortly after the shooting, a man named Lee Harvey Oswald was charged with the crime. Two days later, Oswald was shot dead by a man named Jack Ruby. With so many twists and turns, the story played a bit like a movie.

Many conspiracy theories exist about the Kennedy assassination. Nearly all of them claim that Oswald was not the person responsible. Others say that Oswald killed the president, but he didn't act alone.

Some theories suggest that JFK was killed by the Mafia. Others state that the Freemasons were behind the assassination. Still others blame aliens. A more recent theory linked the crime to a man named Rafael Cruz. He is the father of Ted Cruz, a US senator and 2016 presidential candidate.

President Kennedy riding in his limousine just before he was assassinated.

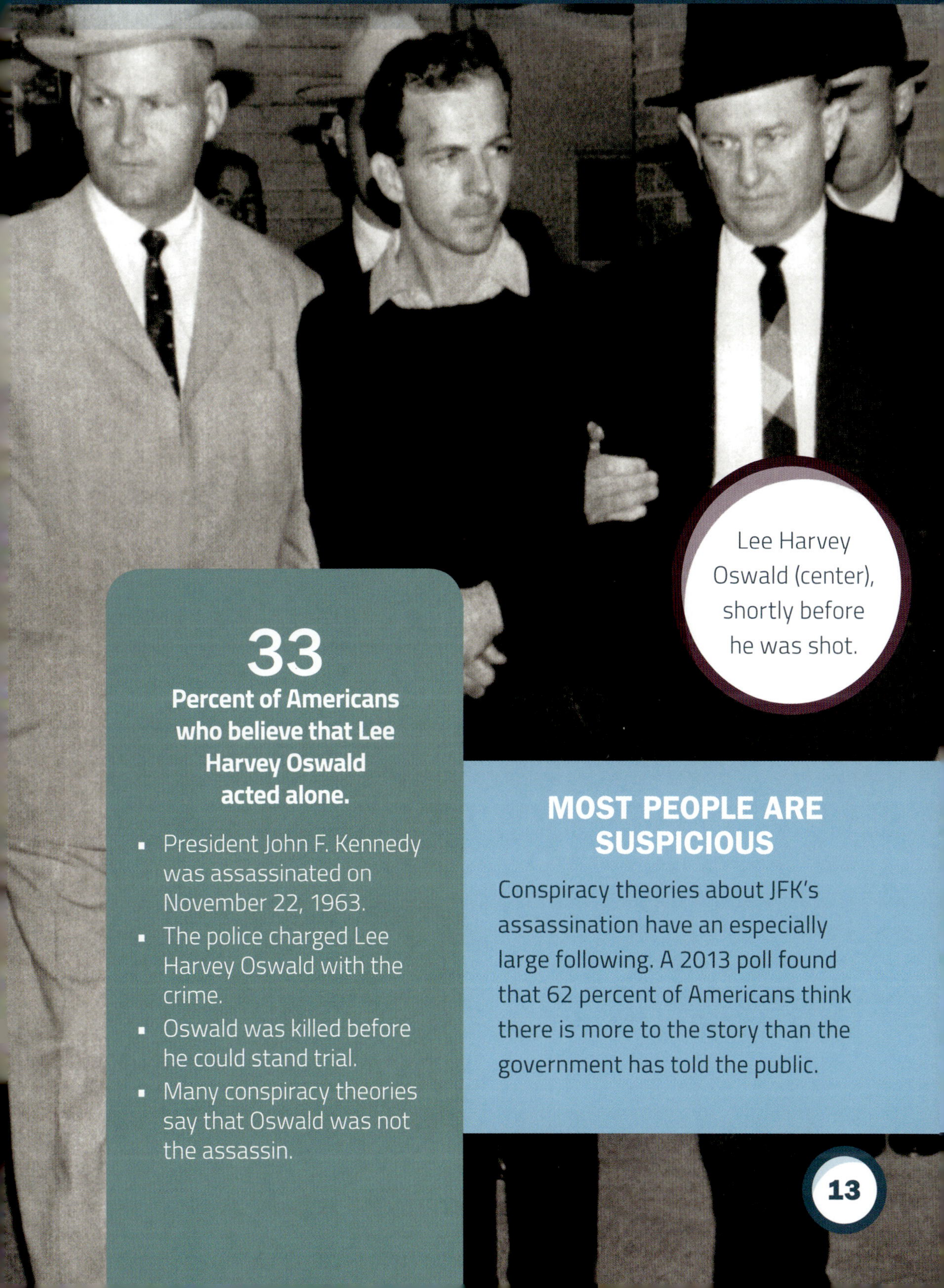

Lee Harvey Oswald (center), shortly before he was shot.

33

Percent of Americans who believe that Lee Harvey Oswald acted alone.

- President John F. Kennedy was assassinated on November 22, 1963.
- The police charged Lee Harvey Oswald with the crime.
- Oswald was killed before he could stand trial.
- Many conspiracy theories say that Oswald was not the assassin.

MOST PEOPLE ARE SUSPICIOUS

Conspiracy theories about JFK's assassination have an especially large following. A 2013 poll found that 62 percent of Americans think there is more to the story than the government has told the public.

6

NASA Faked the Moon Landings

One of the most widely seen videos in history shows the *Apollo 11* moon landing. It was the first time humans had walked on the moon. The date was July 20, 1969. Five more manned missions to the moon took place between then and 1972. Many people have trouble believing these trips were possible. Some refuse to believe they happened.

These conspiracy theorists think the National Aeronautics and Space Administration (NASA) faked the moon landings. They claim that NASA filmed the astronauts on a secret Hollywood film set. Some even think the videos were filmed in Area 51.
This is a place where conspiracy theorists say the government keeps a crashed UFO.

Believers of this theory point to the flag astronaut Buzz Aldrin planted on the moon. The 1969 footage shows the flag moving. The flag could not have moved without airflow. There is no air on the moon. Therefore, the footage must be fake. But scientists have explained that inertia made the flag ripple.

Two astronauts were killed testing equipment for the *Apollo* program. Some people say this tragic accident was part of the hoax. They think the men were executed for threatening to tell the truth about the project.

THINK ABOUT IT

Do you think there is any way to prove that the moon landings actually happened? Why or why not?

6

Percent of Americans who think the moon landings were indeed faked.

- NASA astronauts first landed on the moon on July 20, 1969.
- Five more missions to the moon took place.
- Some people think all of these missions were faked by NASA.
- They think video was filmed on Earth to fool the public.

Astronaut Buzz Aldrin salutes the flag during his historic moonwalk on July 20, 1969.

7

Walt Disney's Body Is Frozen

Walt Disney (right) with his brother, Roy.

Walt Disney died in 1966 from lung cancer. Soon after, a rumor began that his body had been frozen. This theory states that Disney thought doctors might one day find a cure for what killed him. He hoped to be

Walt Disney and his brother, Roy, founded the Disney motion picture company. Walt also founded Disneyland and Walt Disney World. These business ventures were wildly successful during Disney's life. Today the Walt Disney Company is worth billions of dollars.

$200,000

Minimum cost to freeze a dead body at one cryonics company.

- Walt Disney founded the Disney motion picture company and theme parks.
- Following Disney's death in 1966, a rumor started that his body had been frozen.
- Disney was interested in cryogenics.
- People close to Disney have reported that he wanted his body to be frozen.

THE HAPPIEST RESTING PLACE ON EARTH

Many people who believe that Walt Disney's body was frozen have a theory about where it is now. They think his corpse was hidden at Disneyland in California. The most common theory is that Disney's body was placed somewhere beneath Sleeping Beauty's Castle.

brought back to life when this happened.

One reason why this rumor started was Disney's interest in cryogenics. This is the science of how things are affected by very low temperatures. Disney was also interested in the future. The Epcot park at Walt Disney World was his vision for the future. Some people who knew Disney have said that he wanted his body to be frozen. But his family decided to have him cremated instead.

8

Elvis Presley Faked His Own Death

Elvis Presley rose to fame in the 1950s. He became one of the most popular and successful musicians in history. Some of his many hits were "All Shook Up," "Hound Dog," and "Heartbreak Hotel." He was called the King of Rock and Roll. Later that was shortened to the King.

He was also a movie and television star. Some of his movies were *King Creole*, *Jailhouse Rock*, and *Blue Hawaii*. His TV specials were huge hits. More than a billion people watched *Elvis: Aloha from Hawaii* in 1973. He died suddenly in 1977 from a drug overdose.

Elvis was such a big star that he became known by his first name alone. After his death, countless fans had a hard time believing he was gone. One conspiracy theory says that Elvis faked his own death because he was tired of getting so much attention. Another says he did it to escape the Mafia.

Many fans claim to have seen Elvis since his death more than 40 years

25,000

Number of Elvis fans who waited outside his Graceland mansion on the day of his funeral.

- Elvis Presley was a famous musician and actor.
- He died in 1977.
- Some people think Elvis faked his death to escape the spotlight.
- Several fans have reported seeing Elvis alive decades after his death.

ago. Three fans started the Elvis Sighting Society. This group keeps track of people who think they have encountered the singer. People have reported seeing Elvis in places like a Burger King in Kalamazoo, Michigan.

9

Diana, Princess of Wales, Was Murdered

On August 31, 1997, Diana, Princess of Wales, was killed in a car accident in Paris. Paparazzi were chasing her car. They hoped to get photos of the princess with her companion, Dodi Fayed. Diana's driver sped into a tunnel. The car crashed into a wall at high speed.

Diana stood out from the British royal family. She did not always

2.5 billion

Number of people who watched Princess Diana's funeral on television in 1997.

- Diana, Princess of Wales, was beloved by people around the world.
- She did not always act like other members of the royal family.
- Diana was killed in a car crash in 1997 while being chased by paparazzi.
- Many people think the crash was planned by people who wanted the princess dead.

follow the rules that other royals did. Many British people found that refreshing. But members of the royal family didn't. In August 1996, Diana and her husband, Prince Charles, were divorced. In 1997, she was dating Fayed, an Egyptian businessman. Fayed was also killed in the crash.

Some people believe the crash was no accident. They think someone planned it to remove Diana from the public eye. The princess was very popular with the British people and famous around the world. Conspiracy theorists claim that someone paid the driver to crash the car.

Diana, Princess of Wales, with children injured by land mines.

A FLASH OF LIGHT?

Another theory about Diana's death suggests the accident wasn't the driver's fault. People who believe this theory say a flash of light went off inside Diana's car just before the crash. The flash was meant to startle the driver and cause him to lose control of the vehicle.

10 The US Government Was Behind the 9/11 Attacks

The World Trade Center in March 2001.

On September 11, 2001, 19 men hijacked four commercial airplanes and used them to attack the United States. Two planes crashed into the twin towers of the World Trade Center in New York City. A third smashed into the Pentagon in Washington, DC. The fourth was flying to the White House when it crashed into a field in Pennsylvania. The passengers had tried to take back control of the plane.

Some people think the 9/11 attacks were an inside job. They claim the US government was behind the attacks. People who believe this theory don't understand how the towers could have fallen so quickly. The fires caused by the planes had only been burning for a couple of hours. They point out that the amateur pilot who crashed into the

Aerial view of the Pentagon on September 14, 2001.

54

Percent of Americans who believe the government is hiding what they know about 9/11.

- The attacks occurred in the United States after 19 men hijacked four commercial planes.
- Three of the planes crashed into the World Trade Center and the Pentagon. A fourth plane crashed in a Pennsylvania field.
- Conspiracy theories suggest that the US government planned the attacks.
- Believers in these theories don't think science backs up the details of what happened that day.

Pentagon didn't have enough experience to carry out the difficult maneuver. Many people also think the plane that crashed in Pennsylvania was shot down by a US missile.

THINK ABOUT IT

The hijackers were all killed on 9/11. How might someone go about proving whether the US government hired them?

11

Barack Obama Wasn't Born in the United States

Barack Obama became the first African American president of the United States in 2008. The race for president is very tough. Candidates search for anything they can find to discredit each other. Some of Barack Obama's opponents claimed he wasn't born in the United States. If this were true, he couldn't be president. Only natural-born US citizens can do that. This requirement is part of the US Constitution.

43

Number of white men who served as president of the United States before Obama took office.

- Barack Obama became the first African American US president in 2008.
- Only people who were born in the United States are allowed to serve as president.
- Many people who didn't want Obama to win claimed he wasn't eligible to run for the office.
- When Obama produced his birth certificate, some people said it wasn't real.

FORGED!

Some people claimed they had found birth certificates proving that Obama was born in Kenya, not the United States. Close inspection of those documents has shown that they were forged. The state of Hawaii, where Obama was born in 1961, has certified that the birth certificate he provided is genuine.

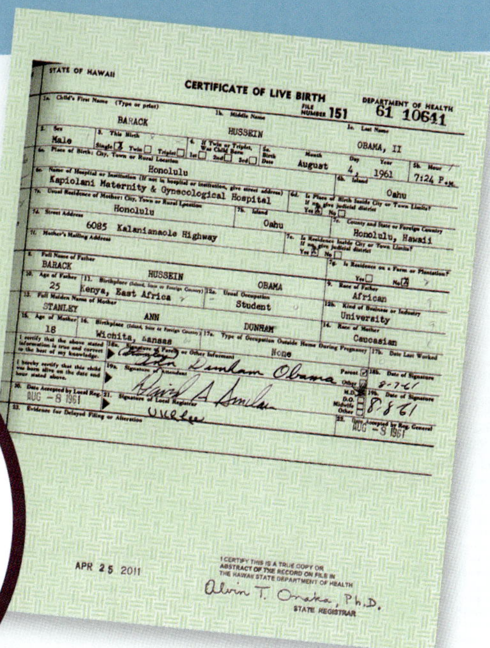

STATE OF HAWAII
CERTIFICATE OF LIVE BIRTH
FILE NUMBER 151 61 10641
DEPARTMENT OF HEALTH

1a. Child's First Name	BARACK
1b. Middle Name	HUSSEIN
1c. Last Name	OBAMA, II
2. Sex	Male
3. This Birth	Single
5a. Birth Date	August 4, 1961
5b. Hour	7:24 P.M.
6a. Place of Birth: City, Town or Rural Location	Honolulu
6b. Island	Oahu
6c. Name of Hospital or Institution	Kapiolani Maternity & Gynecological Hospital
6d. Is Place of Birth Inside City or Town Limits?	Yes
7a. Usual Residence of Mother: City, Town or Rural Location	Honolulu
7b. Island	Oahu
7c. County and State or Foreign Country	Honolulu, Hawaii
7d. Street Address	6085 Kalanianaole Highway
7f. Is Residence Inside City or Town Limits?	Yes
7g. Is Residence on a Farm or Plantation?	No
8. Full Name of Father	BARACK HUSSEIN OBAMA
9. Race of Father	African
10. Age of Father	25
11. Birthplace	Kenya, East Africa
12a. Usual Occupation	Student
12b. Kind of Business or Industry	University
13. Full Maiden Name of Mother	STANLEY ANN DUNHAM
14. Race of Mother	Caucasian
15. Age of Mother	18
16. Birthplace	Wichita, Kansas
17a. Type of Occupation Outside Home During Pregnancy	None
18b. Date of Signature	8-7-61
19b. Date of Signature	8-8-61
20. Date Accepted by Local Reg.	AUG - 8 1961
22. Date Accepted by Reg. General	AUG - 8 1961

APR 25 2011

I CERTIFY THIS IS A TRUE COPY OR ABSTRACT OF THE RECORD ON FILE IN THE HAWAII STATE DEPARTMENT OF HEALTH

Alvin T. Onaka, Ph.D.
STATE REGISTRAR

Barack Obama shown with his father in Hawaii in 1971. And his birth certificate, released by the White House in 2011.

People who didn't like Obama quickly accepted this conspiracy theory. Journalists reported that people were questioning where Obama was born. Even though Obama produced his birth certificate, many believed the document was not genuine. Another theory said that Obama had lost his US citizenship as a child. He had become a citizen of Indonesia instead.

12

The FDA Is Holding Back a Cure for Cancer

Researchers at Sandia National Laboratories working on cancer-fighting drugs.

Making drugs to treat serious illnesses is a profitable business. The longer people need to take medications, the more money a company earns. Many people think drug companies are more interested in treating illnesses than curing them.

This has led to a major conspiracy theory about cancer. Believers think that scientists have already found a cure for cancer. They think drug companies want the cure kept secret. Some people also believe that oncologists, or cancer doctors, are in on the plan. They make money treating patients with cancer. If all of their patients were cured, they would be out of a job.

The Food and Drug Administration (FDA) works with companies that produce all kinds of medications. The FDA tests these drugs to make sure they are safe and effective. Before a drug can be used by people in the United States, the FDA must approve it. Conspiracy theorists think that if the FDA approved a cure for cancer, companies making drugs that treat the disease would go bankrupt.

10

Years it takes the FDA to approve most medications.

- Drug companies make a lot of money off the medications they sell.
- Treating an illness is often more profitable than curing it.
- Before a drug can be sold in the United States, the FDA must approve it.
- Many people think the FDA is hiding the cure for cancer so drug companies won't lose money.

Fact Sheet

- Some conspiracy theorists think Jack the Ripper might have been a woman. One name often linked to the serial killer is Mary Pearcey. In 1890, Pearcey was executed for the murder of her lover's wife and child. They were killed in a manner similar to Jack the Ripper's victims.

- Some survivors of the *Titanic* disaster claimed they heard explosions when the ship began sinking. Some said they never felt the ship hit the iceberg. These reports have led to another conspiracy theory. There are people who believe that *Titanic* was attacked by a German U-boat.

- In 2017, President Donald Trump released 2,800 secret files from the National Archives. The files were about the assassination of John F. Kennedy. Trump chose to keep thousands of other documents private. Historians and conspiracy theorists alike were disappointed.

- Another person thinks there is more to the story of Diana's death. Mohamed Fayed is the father of Dodi Fayed, who also died in the crash. Mohamed has said that his son and Diana were planning to marry. He believes the British royal family did not want the marriage to take place.

Glossary

amateur
A person who does something without a lot of knowledge or experience. A nonprofessional.

anagram
A group of letters that can be arranged to spell more than one word or phrase.

bankrupt
Having more expenses than money to pay them.

conspiracy theory
A belief that an event was caused by, or is controlled by, a group of powerful people.

cryogenics
An area of science that relates to how low temperatures affect living things.

debris
Scattered pieces of things that have been destroyed.

discredit
To harm someone's reputation or cause the person to seem dishonest.

elusive
Hard to track down.

forge
To fake a document or signature to deceive someone.

Freemason
A member of a large organization of men that holds secret ceremonies and helps people.

hijack
To take something over by force, like an airplane or a vehicle.

hoax
Something done on purpose to trick someone.

Mafia
An organized crime group. Also called the mob.

paparazzi
Photographers who follow celebrities to get pictures they can sell.

pen name
A name used by a writer instead of his or her real name.

scam
A dishonest way to make money. A scheme meant to fool people.

For More Information

Books

Kramer, Barbara. *Walt Disney.* National Geographic Readers. Washington, DC: National Geographic Children's Books, 2017.

Labrecque, Ellen. *Who Was Princess Diana?* New York: Grossett and Dunlap, 2017.

Manzanero, Paula K. *Where Is Area 51?* Where Is? New York: Penguin Random House, 2018.

Troupe, Thomas Kingsley. *Titanic's Tragic Journey.* A Fly on the Wall History. North Mankato, MN: Picture Window Books, 2018.

Visit 12StoryLibrary.com

Scan the code or use your school's login at **12StoryLibrary.com** for recent updates about this topic and a full digital version of this book. Enjoy free access to:

- **Digital ebook**
- **Breaking news updates**
- **Live content feeds**
- **Videos, interactive maps, and graphics**
- **Additional web resources**

Note to educators: Visit 12StoryLibrary.com/register to sign up for free premium website access. Enjoy live content plus a full digital version of every 12-Story Library book you own for every student at your school.

Index

About the Author

Tammy Gagne has written more than 200 books for adults and children. She resides in northern New England with her husband and son. One of her favorite pastimes is visiting schools to talk to kids about the writing process.

READ MORE FROM 12-STORY LIBRARY

Every 12-Story Library Book is available in many fomats. For more information, visit 12StoryLibrary.com